AMERICAN GIRL BOOKS ABOUT PUBERTY

PERIOD EDITION

D1714358

DR. LINDA BROOKIE

For all the amazing teen girls out there, who are learning to embrace their bodies and navigate their menstrual cycles. This book is for you.

CONTENTS

Chapter Eight:

Periods and Mental Health

Conclusion

Foreword

For many young girls, the onset of puberty can be an exciting, confusing, and sometimes overwhelming experience. One of the most significant changes that comes with puberty is the onset of menstruation, or periods. Menstruation is a natural and normal process that occurs in the bodies of people with female reproductive systems, and it marks the beginning of a person's reproductive years. However, despite being a natural process, periods are often shrouded in secrecy and stigma, which can lead to confusion, shame, and misinformation.

This book is written for teenage girls who are experiencing or preparing to experience periods. It aims to provide clear, accurate, and accessible information about menstrual health and hygiene, as well as tips and advice for managing the physical and emotional challenges that come with menstruation. Whether you are already having periods or are anticipating their onset, this book is designed to help you understand your body and take control of your menstrual health.

In the following chapters, we'll explore a range of topics related to menstrual health and hygiene, from understanding the menstrual cycle to choosing the right menstrual products, managing symptoms, and talking to others about periods. We'll also cover some of the common concerns and questions that many teens have about periods, such as how they may impact sexual activity, sports participation, and mental health.

While the information in this book is intended to be educational and informative, it is important to remember that everyone's experience with menstruation is different. Some people may have more severe symptoms than others, or may need to use different menstrual products depending on their individual needs. It's also important to remember that menstruation is a normal and natural process, and there is nothing to be ashamed or embarrassed about.

Throughout this book, we'll aim to provide factual and evidence-based information, as well as practical tips and advice that you can use in your everyday life. We'll also highlight some of the common myths and misconceptions about periods, and provide accurate information to help dispel these myths.

Overall, our hope is that this book will serve as a helpful resource for teens who are navigating the world of periods. We believe that by providing accurate information and practical advice, we can help reduce the stigma and confusion surrounding periods, and empower young people to take control of their menstrual health.

- **Dr. Linda Brookie**

Chapter 1

The Menstrual Cycle

People who have a menstrual cycle go through a series of changes in their bodies every month. These changes are part of the menstrual cycle, which is the body's preparation for pregnancy.

Hormones in the body regulate the menstrual cycle. These hormones interact to prepare the uterus for pregnancy and signal the ovaries to release an egg.

The menstrual cycle is divided into four stages: menstruation, follicular phase, ovulation, and luteal phase. The uterine lining is shed during the menstrual phase, resulting in bleeding. This is what is commonly referred to as a period.

The menstrual cycle is a complex physiological process that occurs in the female body over a 28-day period. The cycle is divided into four distinct phases, each with its own distinct features and hormonal changes. Understanding these phases is essential for women who want to better understand and manage their menstrual health.

- **Phase 1: Menstruation (Day 1-5)**
  The menstrual phase begins the menstrual cycle and lasts approximately 3-5 days. The uterus sheds its lining during this phase, resulting in the release of blood, tissue, and other materials from the body. Lower estrogen and progesterone levels during the menstrual phase can cause physical symptoms such as cramps, bloating, and fatigue.

- **Phase 2: Follicular Phase (Day 6-14)**

The follicular phase begins on the first day of menstruation and lasts until ovulation, which typically occurs around day 14. During this phase, the pituitary gland releases follicle-stimulating hormone (FSH) and luteinizing hormone (LH), which stimulate the growth of follicles in the ovaries. The follicles then release estrogen, which helps thicken the uterine lining and prepares the body for pregnancy.

- **Phase 3: Ovulation (Day 14)**
  Ovulation is the briefest phase of the menstrual cycle, lasting only one day. It occurs when the mature follicle in the ovary ruptures and releases an egg. Ovulation is triggered by a surge in luteinizing hormone (LH), which is produced by the pituitary gland. During ovulation, women may experience a slight increase in body temperature, as well as other physical symptoms such as cramping or bloating.

- **Phase 4: Luteal Phase (Day 15-28)**
  The luteal phase begins after ovulation and lasts until the next menstrual period. During this phase, the ruptured follicle in the ovary develops into a structure called the corpus luteum, which releases progesterone. Progesterone helps to thicken the uterine lining and prepare the body for pregnancy. If pregnancy does not occur, the

corpus luteum breaks down, leading to a drop in progesterone levels and the start of a new menstrual cycle.

The menstrual phase begins the menstrual cycle and lasts approximately 3-5 days. The uterus sheds its lining during this phase, resulting in the release of blood, tissue, and other materials from the body. Lower estrogen and progesterone levels during the menstrual phase can cause physical symptoms such as cramps, bloating, and fatigue.

Once the egg is released, it moves through the fallopian tube towards the uterus. This is known as ovulation, and it is the most fertile time in the menstrual cycle.

After ovulation, the body produces another hormone called progesterone. This hormone helps to thicken the lining of the uterus in preparation for a fertilized egg to implant. If the egg is not fertilized, the lining of the uterus will be shed during the next menstrual cycle.

By understanding the menstrual cycle, people can take control of their reproductive health and feel more confident and empowered during their menstrual cycle. In the next chapter, we will be discussing the different types of menstrual products that are available and how to choose the right product for your body.

Brain growth spurt

As a teen, your body is undergoing numerous changes, the most significant of which are occurring in your brain. In fact, your brain grows and changes faster during adolescence than at any other time in your life except when you are a baby.

A "growth spurt" is one of the most significant changes in your brain that occurs during adolescence. This period is marked by an increase in the size and complexity of your brain, which is caused by a surge of hormones and increased neural activity.

During this growth spurt, the brain is refining and strengthening the connections between neurons, which are the cells that transmit information throughout the brain. This process is called "synaptic pruning," and it allows the brain to become more efficient and effective at processing information.

The growth spurt in the brain during adolescence is particularly important because it helps to shape the way that you think, feel, and behave. For example, it is during this time that you are developing your sense of identity and learning to navigate social relationships with peers.

It is also during this time that you are developing important cognitive skills, such as abstract thinking, problem-solving, and planning. These skills will be crucial for your success in school, work, and life in general.

While the growth spurt in the brain during adolescence is an exciting and important time, it can also be a challenging time. The surge of hormones and increased neural activity can lead to heightened emotions, impulsivity, and risk-taking behavior. It is important to remember that these changes are normal and temporary, and that you can take steps to support your brain health during this time.

Eating a balanced diet, getting enough sleep, staying physically active, and engaging in activities that challenge and stimulate your brain, such as reading or solving puzzles, can all help to support your brain's growth and development during this critical period of your life.

First Period

The first period, also known as menarche, is an important milestone in a teenage girl's life. It marks the beginning of menstruation, which is the monthly process by which the body prepares for pregnancy.

The age at which girls experience their first period can vary, but it typically occurs between the ages of 8 and 15. It is important for girls to know that it is normal for the age of their first period to differ from their friends or family members.

The first period may be accompanied by a range of physical and emotional symptoms, including cramping, bloating, mood changes, and anxiety. It is important to know that these symptoms are normal and can be managed with self-care practices, such as rest, hydration, and over-the-counter pain relievers.

It is also important to understand that the first few menstrual cycles may be irregular, resulting in varying bleeding timing and duration. This is normal and can take several months, if not a year, to resolve.

It is critical for adolescent girls to have accurate information about their menstrual cycle and menstrual health. They should be taught how to care for themselves properly during their periods, including how to choose and use menstrual products and maintain good hygiene.

Overall, the first period is a normal and natural part of the female reproductive system, and while it can be frightening, it is an important part of maturing into a young adult.

Hair Growth

One of the changes that many teenage girls experience during puberty is an increase in hair growth, particularly in the pubic and underarm areas. This increase in hair growth is caused by hormonal changes that occur during puberty.

While hair growth is a normal and natural part of puberty, it can also be a source of anxiety and self-consciousness for some girls. It is important to know that everyone's body develops at its own pace, and there is no "right" or "wrong" amount of hair growth.

If you are feeling self-conscious about your hair growth, there are several options for hair removal. Shaving is a common method of hair removal, but it is important to use caution and follow proper shaving techniques to avoid cuts or irritation. Waxing and depilatory creams are other options, but they may be more painful or time-consuming.

It is important to remember that hair growth is a normal part of the development of your body and is nothing to be ashamed of. If you are concerned about your hair growth or any other aspect of your body, it is always a good idea to speak with a trusted adult or healthcare provider who can provide accurate information and support.

Growth Spurt

One of the most visible changes that occur during puberty is the growth spurt. This is a period of rapid growth that is characterized by an increase in height and weight. During this time, teenage girls can grow several inches in a short amount of time.

The growth spurt is caused by puberty-related hormonal changes, specifically the production of estrogen and testosterone. These hormones signal the body to begin developing adult traits such as increased height and muscle mass.

While the growth spurt is a normal and necessary part of puberty, it can be uncomfortable and awkward for some girls. It's important to remember that everyone develops at their own pace, and there's no "right" or "wrong" way to grow.

It is critical to nourish your body during this period of rapid growth by eating a well-balanced diet, staying physically active, and getting enough sleep. This can help to ensure that your body receives the nutrients and energy it requires for healthy growth and development.

If you are experiencing discomfort or pain during your growth spurt, there are several things you can do to manage these symptoms. Stretching and massage can help to alleviate muscle tension and soreness, while over-the-counter pain relievers can help to manage pain and discomfort.

Overall, the growth spurt is a normal and necessary part of puberty, and while it can be difficult, it is an important part of maturing into a young adult.

When it comes to puberty, teenagers frequently wonder what is normal and what is not. It's important to remember that everyone's body develops at their own pace, and there's no "right" or "wrong" way to navigate puberty.

BUT WHAT'S NORMAL?

During puberty, girls can experience a wide range of physical and emotional changes, including breast development, growth spurts, body hair growth, and changes in mood and behavior. It's important to know that these changes are normal and natural, and everyone goes through them at their own pace.

For example, breast development is a common change that many girls experience during puberty. The timing and extent of breast development can vary, but it typically occurs between the ages of 8 and 13. Girls may experience soreness or tenderness in their breasts during this time, but these symptoms usually go away on their own.

Another common change that occurs during puberty is the growth spurt. This is a period of rapid growth that is characterized by an increase in height and weight. The timing and extent of the growth spurt can vary, but it typically occurs between the ages of 8 and 14 for girls. During this time, girls can grow several inches in a short amount of time.

Another common change that occurs during puberty is the growth of body hair. This includes pubic and underarm hair growth, as well as hair growth on the legs and arms. Hair growth can vary in intensity, but it is normal for girls to experience an increase in hair growth during puberty.

Mood and behavioral changes are common during puberty. Anxiety, irritability, and mood swings are examples of such symptoms. These changes are normal and natural and are caused by hormonal fluctuations that occur during puberty.

It's important to remember that, while these changes are normal and natural, they can also be difficult and unpleasant. It is critical that girls have access to accurate information about their bodies and health.

If you have concerns about your physical or emotional changes during puberty, it's important to talk to a trusted adult or healthcare provider who can provide you with accurate information and support. Remember, everyone's body develops at its own pace, and there is no "right" or "wrong" way to go through puberty.

RUBE GOLDBERG MACHINE

A Rube Goldberg machine, which is a complicated machine that performs a simple task, may appear unrelated to hormones. However, there is an intriguing link between the two.

Hormones are chemical messengers that regulate many bodily functions, including growth, metabolism, and reproduction. They are produced by several glands in the body, including the pituitary, thyroid, and adrenal glands.

Hormonal changes play an important role in the physical and emotional changes that teenagers go through during puberty. For example, the hormone estrogen is responsible for female breast development, whereas the hormone testosterone is responsible for male sex development in boys.

Just like a Rube Goldberg machine, the hormonal system is a complex and interconnected system. Each hormone interacts with other hormones and bodily systems to regulate various functions. Any disruption to the hormonal system can have a significant impact on overall health and well-being.

One example of this is the condition known as polycystic ovary syndrome (PCOS), which is a hormonal disorder that affects women. PCOS is characterized by high levels of male hormones, which can cause a range of symptoms such as irregular periods, acne, and hair growth.

Similarly, disruptions to the hormonal system can also affect mood and behavior. For example, fluctuations in the levels of the hormone cortisol, which is released in response to stress, can cause mood swings, anxiety, and depression.

In a way, the hormonal system is like a Rube Goldberg machine, with each hormone playing a specific role in a complex chain of events. Just like a Rube Goldberg machine, any disruption to this system can cause the entire chain to break down, leading to a range of health problems.

Understanding the role of hormones in the body is important for teenagers, especially those going through puberty. It can help them better understand the changes they are experiencing and provide them with the tools they need to maintain their health and well-being.

In conclusion, while the connection between hormones and a Rube Goldberg machine may not seem obvious, there are interesting parallels between the two. Both are complex and interconnected systems that rely on a series of chain reactions to function properly. Understanding the role of hormones in the body is important for teenagers, and can help them navigate the challenges of puberty with confidence and ease.

W-O-M-A-N-?

Let's talk about a wonderful word: WOMAN! Yes, you read that correctly: YOU ARE A WOMAN! Being a woman is also a superpower!

You have the incredible ability as a woman to create and nurture life. Your body is capable of incredible feats, and it is critical to accept and celebrate your individuality.

Being a woman also entails having periods, which can be inconvenient at times, but it's important to remember that it's a completely natural and normal process. Indeed, many cultures around the world regard a girl's first period as a watershed moment in her life.

So, embrace your inner Wonder Woman and celebrate all the amazing things that make you YOU! Don't be afraid to be bold, strong, and confident. And remember, there's nothing more powerful than a woman who knows her worth!

The experience of getting your first period can be different for everyone, but there are some common physical and emotional changes you may notice.

BUT HOW WILL IT FEEL? CAN YOU TELL ME

Physically, you may experience some discomfort or mild cramping in your lower abdomen, which is caused by the muscles of the uterus contracting. You may also notice some changes in your vaginal discharge, which can become thicker and stickier. You might also notice some spotting or light bleeding, which is a sign that your period has started.

Emotionally, you may feel a range of emotions, including excitement, nervousness, and even a little bit of fear. It's completely normal to feel overwhelmed by the changes happening in your body and unsure about what to expect.

One thing to keep in mind is that getting your first period is a completely natural and normal process. It's a sign that your body is growing and changing, and it's a part of the journey to becoming a woman.

If you're feeling anxious or unsure, it can be helpful to talk to someone you trust, like a parent, guardian, or healthcare provider. They can help answer any questions you have and provide you with the support you need during this time.

Remember, every girl goes through this experience, and it's nothing to be ashamed of. You are strong, resilient, and capable of handling whatever comes your way. So take a deep breath, embrace your inner power, and know that you've got this!

Puberty is a complex process that involves many different hormones, each of which plays an important role in the development of your body and its reproductive system.

TESTOSTERONE & ESTROGEN

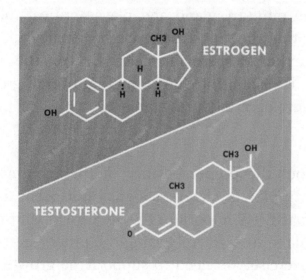

The two main hormones involved in puberty are estrogen and testosterone. Estrogen is the hormone responsible for the development of female sexual characteristics, such as breast development and the onset of menstruation. Testosterone, on the other hand, is the hormone responsible for the development of male sexual characteristics, such as muscle mass and facial hair growth.

In addition to these primary hormones, there are many other hormones that are involved in the puberty process, including luteinizing hormone (LH), follicle-stimulating hormone (FSH), and growth hormone (GH).

LH and FSH are both hormones that are produced by the pituitary gland and play a critical role in regulating the menstrual cycle in females and the production of sperm in males. GH, on the other hand, is responsible for promoting overall growth and development during puberty.

Without the proper balance of these hormones, puberty may be delayed or may not occur at all. That's why it's important to take care of your body and make sure you're getting the proper nutrition and exercise you need to support the growth and development of your body during this important time.

What Is "Early Puberty"?

Early puberty, also known as precocious puberty, is a condition in which puberty begins earlier than the typical age range. For girls, early puberty is defined as the onset of breast development before the age of 8, and for boys, it is defined as the onset of testicular enlargement before the age of 9.

There are many factors that can contribute to early puberty, including genetics, environmental factors, and underlying medical conditions. In some cases, there may be no identifiable cause.

While early puberty may seem like a good thing, as it may make a child appear more mature physically, it can also come with a number of challenges. Children who experience early puberty may feel self-conscious or embarrassed about their physical development, and may be more likely to experience bullying or teasing from their peers.

Early puberty can also have negative health consequences, as it may increase the risk of developing certain health conditions later in life, such as breast cancer in girls and prostate cancer in boys.

If you suspect that your child may be experiencing early puberty, it's important to talk to a healthcare provider. They can help determine the underlying cause and recommend appropriate treatment options, if necessary.

While early puberty can be a challenging experience for children and their families, it's important to remember that every child develops at their own pace, and there is no "right" or "wrong" way to go through puberty. With the right support and care, children who experience early puberty can go on to lead healthy and fulfilling lives.

Chapter Two:

Menstruation is a natural process that girls experience as they enter puberty. The monthly process by which a woman's body prepares for the possibility of pregnancy is known as the menstrual cycle. The menstrual cycle can last between 21 and 35 days, with the average cycle lasting around 28 days. During this time, the body undergoes a series of hormonal changes, causing the ovaries to release an egg, which then travels through the fallopian tubes and into the uterus.

The Menstrual Cycle

The uterine lining thickens during the menstrual cycle in preparation for a fertilized egg. If the egg is not fertilized, the uterine lining is shed as menstrual blood through the vagina. Menstrual blood can range in color and consistency. They should also be prepared with proper menstrual hygiene products, such as pads or tampons.

It is normal for the menstrual cycle to be irregular during the first few years after puberty. However, if a girl experiences severe pain, excessive bleeding, or irregular periods, she should speak with a healthcare provider. Regular gynecological checkups can also help ensure that a girl's reproductive system is healthy and functioning properly. Overall, understanding and taking care of one's menstrual cycle is an important part of maintaining overall health and well-being.

> **What happens in the body each month and how are periods triggered?**

Each month, a complex series of hormonal changes occurs in a woman's body in preparation for the possibility of pregnancy. These hormonal changes are controlled by the hypothalamus and pituitary gland in the brain, which produce hormones that signal the ovaries to produce and release eggs.

The menstrual cycle begins on the first day of menstrual bleeding and lasts until the start of the next menstrual period. During the first half of the menstrual cycle, which is known as the follicular phase, the hormone estrogen is produced by the ovaries. This causes the lining of the uterus to thicken in preparation for a fertilized egg. At the same time, the pituitary gland produces follicle-stimulating hormone (FSH), which triggers the growth and development of follicles in the ovaries.

Each follicle contains an egg, but only one follicle will reach maturity and release an egg.

Around day 14 of the menstrual cycle, a surge in luteinizing hormone (LH) from the pituitary gland triggers ovulation, which is the release of the mature egg from the ovary. The egg then travels through the fallopian tube towards the uterus. If the egg is fertilized by a sperm, it will implant in the lining of the uterus and pregnancy will occur. If the egg is not fertilized, it will disintegrate and be absorbed by the body.

After ovulation, the empty follicle in the ovary develops into a structure called the corpus luteum, which produces the hormone progesterone. Progesterone helps to maintain the thickened lining of the uterus and prepares it for the implantation of a fertilized egg. If pregnancy does not occur, the corpus luteum will break down and the levels of estrogen and progesterone will decrease, causing the lining of the uterus to shed. This shedding of the uterine lining is what causes menstrual bleeding, which is the start of a new menstrual cycle.

Overall, the menstrual cycle is a complex process that is controlled by a delicate balance of hormones. Any disruptions in this balance can affect the regularity of the menstrual cycle, which is why it is important for women to pay attention to their menstrual cycles and seek medical attention if they experience any irregularities.

> ## Managing Menstrual Symptoms

For adolescent girls, their first menstrual cycle can be both exciting and frightening. While menstruation is a natural process that marks a girl's reproductive maturity, it can also be accompanied by unpleasant symptoms that are unfamiliar and unsettling. These symptoms can include cramping, bloating, mood changes, headaches, and fatigue, among others. Understanding how to manage these symptoms is an important part of maintaining overall health and well-being during the menstrual cycle.

The good news is that there are several strategies that teen girls can use to manage menstrual symptoms and improve their quality of life during their periods. One of the most effective ways to manage menstrual symptoms is through lifestyle changes. Teen girls can try regular exercise, a healthy diet, and stress reduction techniques to alleviate menstrual symptoms. Exercise has been shown to reduce menstrual pain and cramping, as well as improve mood and reduce fatigue. A healthy diet that is rich in fruits, vegetables, whole grains, and lean protein can also help to alleviate menstrual symptoms by reducing inflammation in the body and providing the nutrients needed for optimal health. Stress reduction techniques, such as meditation, deep breathing, or yoga, can also be helpful in managing menstrual symptoms by reducing anxiety and improving relaxation.

For those experiencing severe menstrual symptoms, over-the-counter pain relievers can also be effective. Nonsteroidal anti-inflammatory drugs (NSAIDs), such as ibuprofen or naproxen, can help to reduce menstrual pain and cramping, as well as alleviate headaches and reduce inflammation in the body. Teen girls should always talk to their healthcare provider or a trusted adult before taking any new medication, especially if they have a history of gastrointestinal issues or other medical conditions.

Hormonal birth control can be an effective option for teen girls experiencing severe menstrual symptoms that do not respond to lifestyle changes or over-the-counter medications. Hormonal birth control, such as the pill, patch, or ring, works by regulating the hormonal fluctuations that occur during the menstrual cycle, which can aid in the reduction of menstrual pain, the regulation of periods, and the improvement of mood. Teen girls should discuss the risks and benefits of hormonal birth control with their healthcare provider or a trusted adult to determine whether it is the best option for them.

Overall, managing menstrual symptoms is an important part of maintaining overall health and well-being for teen girls. By making lifestyle changes, using over-the-counter medications, or using hormonal birth control, teen girls can improve their quality of life during their menstrual cycles and reduce the impact of menstrual symptoms on daily activities. Teen girls should always talk to a trusted adult or healthcare provider about their menstrual symptoms and any concerns they may have about managing them, as there are a variety of options available to help manage menstrual symptoms and improve overall health.

> **Menstrual Cramps**

For Menstrual cramps are a common and unpleasant part of the menstrual cycle for many adolescent girls. Cramps can cause mild discomfort to severe pain and disrupt daily activities such as school, work, and socializing. Understanding the causes of menstrual cramps and how to manage them can help teen girls reduce pain and improve their quality of life during their periods.

Menstrual cramps occur when the uterus contracts during menstruation to shed its lining. These contractions can cause pain and discomfort in the lower abdomen, back, and thighs. Menstrual cramp severity varies from person to person and is influenced by factors such as age, hormonal changes, and underlying medical conditions.

While menstrual cramps are a normal part of the menstrual cycle, there are several strategies that teen girls can use to manage them. One of the most effective ways to manage menstrual cramps is through lifestyle changes. Regular exercise, a healthy diet, and stress reduction techniques can all help to alleviate menstrual cramps. Exercise has been shown to reduce menstrual pain and cramping, as well as improve mood and reduce fatigue. A healthy diet that is rich in fruits, vegetables, whole grains, and lean protein can also help to alleviate menstrual cramps by reducing inflammation in the body and providing the nutrients needed for optimal health. Stress reduction techniques, such as meditation, deep breathing, or yoga, can also be helpful in managing menstrual cramps by reducing anxiety and improving relaxation.

Over-the-counter pain relievers can also be effective in managing menstrual cramps. Nonsteroidal anti-inflammatory drugs (NSAIDs), such as ibuprofen or naproxen, can help to reduce menstrual pain and cramping, as well as alleviate headaches and reduce inflammation in the body. Teen girls should always talk to their healthcare provider or a trusted adult before taking any new medication, especially if they have a history of gastrointestinal issues or other medical conditions.

For teen girls experiencing severe menstrual cramps that do not respond to lifestyle changes or over-the-counter medications, hormonal birth control can be an effective option for managing symptoms. Hormonal birth control, such as the pill, patch, or ring, works by regulating the hormonal fluctuations that occur during the menstrual cycle, which can help to reduce menstrual cramps, regulate periods, and improve mood. Teen girls should talk to their healthcare provider or a trusted adult about the risks and benefits of hormonal birth control and whether it is the right option for them.

In addition to these strategies, there are also a variety of at-home remedies that can help alleviate menstrual cramps. Heat therapy, such as using a heating pad or taking a warm bath, can help to relax the muscles in the uterus and reduce cramping. Massaging the lower abdomen or using essential oils such as lavender or peppermint oil can also help to reduce pain and discomfort.

It is important for teen girls to understand that menstrual cramps are a normal part of the menstrual cycle, but there are many strategies that can be used to manage them. By making lifestyle changes, using over-the-counter medications, or using hormonal birth control, teen girls can improve their quality of life during their menstrual cycles and reduce the impact of menstrual cramps on daily activities. Teen girls should always talk to a trusted adult or healthcare provider about their menstrual cramps and any concerns they may have about managing them, as there are a variety of options available to help manage menstrual cramps and improve overall health.

> **Your Emotions**

Many teen girls experience mood swings during their periods. Hormonal changes during the menstrual cycle can affect neurotransmitters in the brain, resulting in mood, behavior, and emotional well-being changes. Understanding the causes of mood changes during periods and developing coping strategies can help adolescent girls feel more in control of their emotions and improve their overall quality of life.

The menstrual cycle is a complex process that involves a delicate balance of hormones, including estrogen, progesterone, and testosterone. These hormones can have a significant impact on neurotransmitters in the brain, including serotonin and dopamine, which regulate mood, behavior, and emotional well-being. For many teen girls, the fluctuation of these hormones during their menstrual cycle can lead to mood changes, such as irritability, anxiety, depression, or mood swings.

In addition to hormonal changes, other factors can also contribute to mood changes during periods. Stress, lack of sleep, poor nutrition, and underlying mental health conditions, such as anxiety or depression, can all exacerbate mood changes during periods. It is important for teen girls to pay attention to their overall physical and emotional well-being, and to seek help from a healthcare provider or trusted adult if they are experiencing persistent or severe mood changes.

There are several strategies that can help manage mood changes during periods. Regular exercise, healthy eating habits, and stress reduction techniques, such as deep breathing or meditation, can all help to improve mood and reduce stress. Getting enough sleep and maintaining a consistent sleep schedule can also help to regulate mood and improve emotional well-being.

For teen girls experiencing severe or persistent mood changes during periods, hormonal birth control can be an effective option for managing symptoms. Hormonal birth control works by regulating the hormonal fluctuations that occur during the menstrual cycle, which can help to reduce mood swings, anxiety, and depression. Teen girls should talk to their healthcare provider or a trusted adult about the risks and benefits of hormonal birth control and whether it is the right option for them.

It is also important for teen girls to practice self-care during their menstrual cycles. This can include engaging in activities that they enjoy, spending time with friends and family, or taking time to relax and unwind. Engaging in activities that promote relaxation and stress reduction, such as taking a warm bath, reading a book, or listening to music, can also be helpful in managing mood changes during periods.

Finally, teen girls should remember that mood swings during periods are a normal part of the menstrual cycle. Many girls experience mood swings during their periods, and they should not be ashamed or embarrassed about their feelings. If mood changes are interfering with daily activities or causing significant distress, it is critical to seek support and guidance from a healthcare provider or trusted adult. .

In conclusion, mood changes during periods are a common experience for many teen girls. Understanding the causes of mood changes during periods and learning strategies to manage them can help teen girls feel more in control of their emotions and improve their overall quality of life. By practicing self-care, seeking support from a healthcare provider or trusted adult, and taking steps to manage stress and improve emotional well-being, teen girls can effectively manage mood changes during periods and live their best lives.

➢ Other Symptoms

Aside from cramps and mood swings, there are a number of other symptoms that can occur during a menstrual cycle. These symptoms can vary in severity and duration, but they can be uncomfortable and interfere with daily activities for many adolescent girls. Understanding these symptoms and developing coping mechanisms can help adolescent girls feel more in control of their bodies and improve their overall quality of life.

One common symptom of menstruation is bloating and water retention. During a menstrual cycle, hormonal changes can cause the body to retain water, leading to bloating, swelling, and discomfort. Eating a healthy, balanced diet that is low in salt and high in fruits and vegetables can help to reduce bloating and water retention. Staying hydrated and avoiding caffeine and alcohol can also help to reduce these symptoms.

Fatigue and low energy are also common symptoms during a menstrual cycle. Hormonal changes can cause fatigue and make it difficult to feel alert and focused. Getting enough rest and sleep during this time is crucial. Engaging in low-intensity physical activity, such as yoga or walking, can also help to reduce fatigue and improve energy levels.

Another symptom of menstruation is acne and skin changes. Hormonal changes during the menstrual cycle can cause oil production to increase, leading to acne and other skin changes. Keeping the skin clean and moisturized, avoiding harsh skincare products, and using non-comedogenic makeup can help to reduce the appearance of acne and other skin changes.

Headaches and migraines are also common menstrual cycle symptoms. Hormonal changes can cause headaches and migraines, which can be incapacitating and interfere with daily activities. Ibuprofen and other over-the-counter pain relievers can help reduce headache and migraine symptoms. Regular exercise, stress reduction techniques, and adequate sleep can also aid in the prevention of headaches and migraines.

Finally, menstrual bleeding is a common symptom of menstruation. Bleeding can vary in duration and flow, but for many teen girls, it can be heavy and uncomfortable. Using sanitary products, such as pads or tampons, can help to manage bleeding and prevent leaks. Changing sanitary products regularly and maintaining good hygiene can also help to prevent infection and odor.

In conclusion, menstruation can cause several uncomfortable symptoms for teen girls. Understanding these symptoms and learning strategies to manage them can help to improve overall physical and emotional well-being. By eating a healthy diet, getting enough rest and sleep, engaging in physical activity, using non-comedogenic skincare products, and using sanitary products, teen girls can effectively manage these symptoms and live their best lives. If symptoms are persistent or severe, it is important to talk to a healthcare provider or trusted adult for support and guidance.

> **Tips to Manage Menstrual Symptoms**

Managing menstrual symptoms can be challenging, but there are several tips and strategies that teen girls can use to alleviate discomfort and improve their overall well-being.

Here are some tips and advice for managing menstrual symptoms:

- **Manage cramps:** Apply heat to the lower abdomen, take over-the-counter pain relievers such as ibuprofen, and engage in low-intensity physical activity, such as walking or yoga.

- **Address mood changes:** Practice stress-reducing techniques, such as deep breathing or meditation, maintain a healthy sleep schedule, and engage in physical activity to improve mood and reduce anxiety.
- **Reduce bloating and water retention**: Eat a healthy, balanced diet that is low in salt and high in fruits and vegetables, stay hydrated, and avoid caffeine and alcohol.
- **Combat fatigue:** Get enough rest and sleep, engage in physical activity to improve energy levels, and prioritize self-care practices such as taking a warm bath or reading a book.
- **Address acne and skin changes:** Keep the skin clean and moisturized, avoid harsh skincare products, and use non-comedogenic makeup.
- **Reduce headaches and migraines:** Take over-the-counter pain relievers such as ibuprofen, practice stress-reducing techniques, and engage in regular physical activity.
- **Manage menstrual bleeding:** Use sanitary products, such as pads or tampons, change them regularly, and maintain good hygiene.

In addition to these suggestions, there are a number of home remedies that can help to relieve menstrual symptoms. Heat applied to the lower abdomen can help to relieve cramps, while soaking in a warm bath can help to relax the body and relieve tension. Herbal teas, such as ginger or chamomile, can also help to alleviate menstrual symptoms.

Menstrual symptoms can be effectively managed with over-the-counter medications such as nonsteroidal anti-inflammatory drugs (NSAIDs) such as ibuprofen or naproxen. These medications work by reducing inflammation and pain and are completely safe when used as prescribed. Before beginning any new medication, always consult with a healthcare provider or a trusted adult.

It is important to note that if menstrual symptoms are persistent or severe, it is important to talk to a healthcare provider or trusted adult for support and guidance. They may recommend other treatment options, such as hormonal birth control or prescription pain relievers, to alleviate symptoms.

In conclusion, managing menstrual symptoms requires a combination of self-care practices, home remedies, and over-the-counter medications. By understanding the various symptoms of menstruation and taking proactive steps to address them, teen girls can alleviate discomfort and improve their overall well-being.

Chapter Three:

Navigating the world of menstrual products as a teen girl can be daunting. With so many options available, determining which products are best for you can be difficult. Choosing the right menstrual product, on the other hand, is an important decision that can affect your comfort, hygiene, and overall well-being during your period.

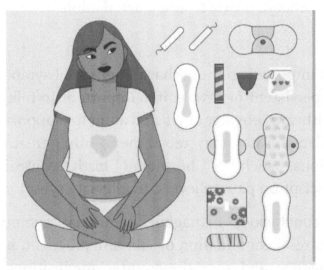

In this chapter, we will explore the various menstrual products available, including pads, tampons, menstrual cups, and period underwear. We will discuss the benefits and drawbacks of each option, as well as provide tips for selecting the product that is best suited for your individual needs.

Choosing the right menstrual product is a personal decision, and there is no one-size-fits-all solution. Some girls prefer pads for their ease of use and reliability, while others prefer tampons for their convenience and discreetness. Menstrual cups and period underwear are newer options that have gained popularity in recent years due to their eco-friendliness and long-term cost-effectiveness.

Whatever menstrual product you choose, it is critical to understand how to use it correctly to ensure maximum comfort and hygiene. By the end of this chapter, you will have a better understanding of the various menstrual products on the market and will be able to make an informed decision that is right for you.

Below is a table of different Menstrual Products, along with their pros and cons:

Menstrual Product	Pros	Cons
Pads	Easy to use, available in various sizes and absorbencies, can be worn with any type of underwear	May feel bulky, can shift or move during physical activity, can cause skin irritation
Tampons	Convenient and discreet, allow for physical activity and swimming, come in various absorbencies	Can be difficult to insert and remove, may increase risk of toxic shock syndrome (TSS) if left in for too long, not recommended for light flow
Menstrual cups	Reusable, eco-friendly, can be worn for up to 12 hours, available in various sizes	May require practice to insert and remove, can be messy to empty and

		clean, not recommended for those with an IUD
Period Underwear	Reusable, eco-friendly, can be worn as a backup or on their own for light to moderate flow, comfortable	May feel bulky or hot, can be expensive upfront, may not provide enough protection for heavy flow

Pads are a popular option for those who want something simple and easy to use. They are available in a variety of sizes and absorbencies to accommodate individual needs and can be worn with any type of underwear. Pads, on the other hand, can be bulky and shift during physical activity, causing discomfort and potential leaks. They can also cause skin irritation, especially when worn for long periods of time.

Tampons are a convenient and discrete option for those who prefer greater mobility. They are available in a variety of absorbencies and can be worn while exercising or swimming. Tampons, on the other hand, can be difficult to insert and remove and, if left in for too long, may increase the risk of

TSS. They are not recommended for light flow because they can be damaged.

Menstrual cups are a newer option that has gained popularity in recent years due to their environmental friendliness and low cost. They are reusable and can be worn for up to 12 hours, making them an ideal choice for those who lead hectic lives. Menstrual cups, on the other hand, can be difficult to insert and remove, and they can be messy to empty and clean. They are also not advised for those who have an IUD.

Another newer option that has gained popularity in recent years is period underwear. They are reusable and can be worn alone or as a backup for light to moderate flow. They are also comfortable and environmentally friendly. They can, however, feel bulky or hot, and they may not provide enough protection for heavy flow. They are capable.

Ultimately, the choice of menstrual product is a personal decision that depends on individual preferences and needs. It is important to understand the pros and cons of each option in order to make an informed decision that is right for you.

Choosing the right menstrual product can feel overwhelming, especially for teenage girls who are just starting their menstrual journey. Here are some tips to help you choose the right menstrual product for you:

1. **Consider your flow:** The first step in choosing the right menstrual product is to consider your flow. If you have a heavy flow, you may need a product with a higher absorbency level, such as a thicker pad or a menstrual cup. If you have a light flow, you may be able to use a thinner pad or a tampon.

2. **Think about your lifestyle:** Your lifestyle is another important factor to consider when choosing a menstrual product. If you are an athlete or enjoy swimming, you may want to consider tampons or menstrual cups, as they allow for more freedom of movement. If you prefer a low-maintenance option, pads or period underwear may be a better fit.

3. **Consider your comfort level:** Comfort is key when it comes to menstrual products. You want to choose a product that you feel comfortable wearing throughout the day. Some girls may prefer the feeling of a pad, while others may prefer the convenience of a tampon or menstrual cup.

4. **Evaluate cost:** Menstrual products can be expensive, so it's important to evaluate the

cost when choosing a product. While some products may be more expensive upfront, they may be more cost-effective in the long run, such as menstrual cups and period underwear.

5. **Do your research:** It's important to do your research when choosing a menstrual product. Read reviews from other girls and women who have tried the product, and watch instructional videos on how to use it properly.

6. **Experiment:** It may take some trial and error to find the right menstrual product for you. Don't be afraid to try different options until you find the one that works best for your body and lifestyle.

Remember, choosing the right menstrual product is a personal decision. Don't feel pressured to use a certain product just because your friends or family members use it. Take the time to evaluate your needs and preferences, and choose the product that makes you feel most comfortable and confident during your period.

Chapter Four:

Talking About Periods

Talking about periods can be awkward and embarrassing for many adolescent girls. It's understandable to feel this way, given that menstruation has long been stigmatized and taboo in society. However, because periods are a natural part of the female reproductive system, it is critical to have open and honest conversations about them.

Education is the first step in removing the stigma associated with menstruation. Because they don't fully understand what is going on in their bodies, many girls may feel embarrassed or ashamed of their periods. We can empower girls to feel confident and comfortable with their bodies by providing period education and information.

It's also important to create a safe space for girls to talk about their periods without fear of judgment or ridicule. By normalizing the conversation around periods, we can help girls feel more comfortable seeking help and advice when they need it.

We will discuss periods in this chapter, including what they are, how they work, and what to expect. We will also go over the various types of menstrual products available and offer advice on how to choose the best one for you. In addition, we will address common concerns and questions about periods that teenage girls may have, such as irregular periods and period cramps.

We hope that by providing accurate and comprehensive period information, we can help teenage girls feel more confident and at ease with their bodies. We also hope to dispel period stigma so that girls can have open and honest conversations about their menstrual health without fear or shame.

> ➤ **How to talk to friends, family and health care providers about your menstrual health:**

Talking about periods can be uncomfortable for many people, but it's important to have open and honest conversations about menstrual health with friends, family, and healthcare providers. Here are some tips for navigating these conversations:

1. *Be honest: When discussing periods with others, it's important to be honest about your experiences and any concerns you may have. By being open and honest, you can encourage others to do the same and create a safe space for conversation.*

2. *Use proper terminology:* *It's important to use proper terminology when discussing periods, as it can help to destigmatize the conversation. Using words like "menstruation" and "period" instead of slang terms can help to normalize the conversation and promote open dialogue.*

3. *Seek out trusted individuals:* *If you're unsure of how to talk about periods with someone, seek out trusted individuals, such as family members or close friends. They may have valuable insights and advice to offer.*

4. *Educate yourself:* *Educating yourself about menstrual health can help you to feel more confident in discussing periods with others. You can do this by reading books or articles on the topic, attending educational workshops or classes, or speaking with a healthcare provider.*

5. *Be respectful:* *When discussing periods with others, it's important to be respectful of their experiences and perspectives. Everyone's experience with periods is unique, and it's important to acknowledge and respect those differences.*

6. *Advocate for yourself:* *If you're experiencing menstrual health issues, it's important to advocate for yourself and seek out the support and care you need. This may mean speaking*

with a healthcare provider, seeking out support groups or resources, or simply sharing your experiences with others.

7. ***Normalize the conversation:*** *By normalizing the conversation around periods, we can break down the stigma surrounding menstruation and create a more open and accepting society. This can be done by having conversations about periods in everyday settings, such as at school or in the workplace.*

In conclusion, talking about periods can be uncomfortable, but it's important to have open and honest conversations about menstrual health with friends, family, and healthcare providers. By following these tips, we can create a more supportive and accepting society that values and prioritizes menstrual health.

DOCTOR Q & A
Dr. Rebecca Coleman

Gynecologist

Q: What are some common menstrual symptoms?

A: Common menstrual symptoms include cramps, bloating, mood changes, and fatigue.

Q: What are some different types of menstrual products?

A: Some different types of menstrual products include tampons, pads, menstrual cups, and period panties.

Q: How can you choose the right menstrual product for you?

A: To choose the right menstrual product for you, consider factors such as flow level, personal preferences, and lifestyle needs.

Q: What are some home remedies for managing menstrual symptoms?

A: Some home remedies for managing menstrual symptoms include using heat therapy, practicing relaxation techniques, and incorporating certain foods into your diet.

Q: How can you talk to friends and family about periods?

A: To talk to friends and family about periods, be honest, use proper terminology, seek out trusted individuals, and be respectful of differences in experiences and perspectives.

Q: What are some tips for talking to healthcare providers about menstrual health?

A: Some tips for talking to healthcare providers about menstrual health include being honest and open about your experiences, advocating for yourself, and asking questions to clarify any concerns or uncertainties.

Q: What is a menstrual cup and how does it work?

A: A menstrual cup is a small, flexible cup made of silicone or rubber that is inserted into the vagina to collect menstrual fluid. It works by creating a seal against the vaginal walls, preventing leakage and collecting fluid for up to 12 hours.

Q: How can you manage period cramps?

A: To manage period cramps, try using heat therapy, practicing relaxation techniques, taking over-the-counter pain medications, or incorporating certain foods into your diet.

Q: What should you do if you experience irregular periods?

A: If you experience irregular periods, it's important to speak with a healthcare provider to rule out any underlying medical conditions and develop a plan for managing your menstrual health.

Q: How can you break down the stigma surrounding periods?

A: To break down the stigma surrounding periods, we can normalize the conversation around menstruation, use proper terminology, educate ourselves and others, and advocate for menstrual health as a priority in society.

History:

Menstruation has been a topic of discussion throughout history, with various cultures having different attitudes and beliefs surrounding it. In ancient Egypt, menstruating women were considered to be impure and were not allowed to enter temples or other sacred spaces. In ancient Greece, menstruation was seen as a necessary evil and women were thought to be at their most dangerous and irrational during their periods. In some cultures, menstruation was even seen as a curse or punishment.

However, attitudes towards menstruation have evolved over time, with efforts to break down the stigma and taboo surrounding it. In the early 20th century, the invention of commercial menstrual products such as disposable pads and tampons revolutionized menstrual hygiene and made it more convenient for women to manage their periods. Today, there are even more menstrual product options available, including menstrual cups and period panties.

"It's time to end the shame and secrecy surrounding periods and make menstrual health a priority for all women." - Padma Lakshmi

Chapter Five:

Periods and Sex

For many young people, puberty brings a host of changes, including the onset of menstruation and the development of sexual feelings and desires. As teens navigate these new experiences and learn more about their bodies, it's important to understand how periods and sex intersect.

In this chapter, we will explore the ways in which periods and sex are related, including how periods can affect sexual activity and how to manage menstruation during sex. We will also discuss common concerns and questions that teens may have about periods and sex, such as whether it's safe to have sex during menstruation and how to talk to a partner about periods.

It's important to remember that everyone's experience with periods and sex is unique, and there is no single "correct" way to approach these topics. Understanding the fundamentals and learning how to communicate with partners and health care providers, on the other hand, can help young people feel more confident and empowered about their sexual and reproductive health.

We will provide factual information and practical tips to help teens navigate the complex and sometimes confusing world of periods and sex throughout this chapter. We'll also look at some of the cultural and social attitudes that influence how people think about periods and sex, as well as how to challenge negative stereotypes and myths.

Young people can gain a better understanding and appreciation for their bodies and sexuality by learning more about periods and sex. Whether you are just beginning to explore your sexual feelings or have been sexually active for a while, this chapter will provide you with valuable insights and guidance to help you make informed choices and stay healthy and happy.

➢ How do Periods affect Sexual Activity?

Periods can affect sexual activity in a number of ways, both physically and emotionally.

Physically, many people experience changes in their bodies during their period that can make sexual activity uncomfortable or even painful. For example, menstrual cramps can be intense and may make it difficult to relax during sex. Additionally, some people experience bloating or other physical discomfort during their period that can make them feel self-conscious or less interested in sexual activity.

Emotionally, some people may feel more irritable or moody during their period, which can impact their desire for sex or their ability to feel emotionally connected with a partner. Additionally, some people may feel self-conscious about their period, either because they are worried about leaking or because they feel embarrassed about the idea of having sex while menstruating.

Despite these challenges, many people find that they are still able to enjoy sexual activity during their period. Some people even find that sex can help to alleviate menstrual cramps and other physical discomforts.

If you are experiencing discomfort or other issues related to sex during your period, there are a number of things you can do to manage these symptoms. For example, you may want to try using a different sexual position that is more comfortable for you during your period, or you may want to consider using a menstrual product such as a menstrual cup or tampon to help prevent leakage during sex.

Additionally, it can be helpful to communicate openly with your partner about your needs and concerns. Letting your partner know that you are on your period and discussing any physical or emotional symptoms you are experiencing can help to create a more supportive and understanding environment for sexual activity.

Ultimately, the most important thing is to listen to your body and do what feels right for you. If you are not feeling up for sex during your period, that is perfectly okay. There is no one "right" way to approach sex and menstruation, and it's important to prioritize your own needs and comfort above all else.

Tips & Advice

Managing your period during sex can be a challenge, but there are a number of tips and tricks you can use to make the experience more comfortable and enjoyable. Here are some suggestions:

1. **Use menstrual products:** One of the most important things you can do to manage your period during sex is to use a menstrual product, such as a tampon or menstrual cup. These products can help to prevent leakage and keep you feeling more comfortable during sex. It's important to choose a product that is comfortable for you and that you feel confident using.

2. **Change your position:** Some sexual positions may be more comfortable than others during your period. For example, you may want to avoid positions that put pressure on your abdomen, such as missionary or doggy style. Instead, try positions that allow you to control the depth and angle of penetration, such as woman-on-top or spooning.

3. **Communicate with your partner:** It can be helpful to communicate openly with your partner about your period and any concerns

you may have about sex. Letting your partner know that you are on your period and discussing any physical or emotional symptoms you are experiencing can help to create a more supportive and understanding environment for sexual activity.

4. **Take a break:** If you are experiencing discomfort or other issues related to sex during your period, it's important to listen to your body and take a break if needed. There is no shame in taking a break from sex during your period if you are not feeling up for it.

5. **Use a towel:** If you are concerned about leakage during sex, you may want to place a towel underneath you to help absorb any blood. This can help to prevent staining and make cleanup easier.

6. **Consider shower sex:** Some people find that having sex in the shower during their period can be more comfortable and less messy. The water can help to wash away any blood and make cleanup easier.

7. **Practice good hygiene:** It's important to practice good hygiene during your period, especially if you are engaging in sexual activity. Make sure to wash your hands and genitals before and after sex, and consider taking a shower or bath afterwards to help clean up any blood.

Overall, managing your period during sex can be a challenge, but it's important to remember that it is a normal part of life and nothing to be ashamed of. By using menstrual products, communicating with your partner, and practicing good hygiene, you can help to make the experience more comfortable and enjoyable. Remember to listen to your body and do what feels right for you.

Questions & Answers

Dr. Sarah Cody

Q: Can I have sex while on my period?

A: Yes, you can have sex while on your period. It is, however, critical to use protection to avoid pregnancy and sexually transmitted infections.

Q: Will having sex make my period shorter?

A: No, having sex during your period will not make it shorter.

Q: Can I get pregnant while on my period?

A: Yes, it is possible to get pregnant while on your period, although it is less likely. It is important to use contraception to prevent unwanted pregnancy.

Q: Can I use a tampon during sex?

A: It is not recommended to use a tampon during sex, as it can increase the risk of infection and discomfort. It is best to use other menstrual products like a menstrual cup or pad.

Q: Is it normal to have cramps during sex while on my period?

A: It is not uncommon to experience cramps during sex while on your period. Changing positions or taking a break can help alleviate discomfort.

Q: Can I still have an orgasm during my period?

AYes, you can still have an orgasm during your period. Some women, however, may feel uncomfortable or prefer not to engage in sexual activity during this time.

Q: Can I masturbate during my period?

A: Yes, it is safe to masturbate during your period. Using menstrual products like a menstrual cup or pad can help prevent leakage.

Chapter Six:

Menstrual Health and Hygiene

Managing your menstrual cycle as an adolescent girl can be difficult. Menstruation is a normal and natural process that every woman goes through, but it can be uncomfortable, cause leakage, and cause hygiene issues. To avoid infections and other complications, it is critical to maintain good menstrual health and hygiene. Proper menstrual hygiene practices can assist you in effectively managing your periods, allowing you to go about your daily activities without interruption. Unfortunately, many teenage girls lack access to proper menstrual hygiene resources, leading to negative effects on their health and well-being. This chapter aims to provide information and tips on menstrual health and hygiene for teenage girls. By taking care of our menstrual health, we can improve our overall health and quality of life. This chapter will cover topics such as choosing menstrual products, managing symptoms, and talking to friends and family about periods. By the end of this chapter, you will have a better understanding of menstrual health and hygiene, empowering you to take control of your menstrual cycle.

> ➤ **What are the Basics of Menstrual Hygiene?**

Maintaining good menstrual hygiene is crucial for preventing infections and other complications during your period. Here are some basic tips for menstrual hygiene:

A. **Change your menstrual products regularly:** Whether you use pads, tampons, or menstrual cups, it's important to change them regularly to prevent leakage and infection. Aim to change your product every 4-6 hours, or more often if you have heavy bleeding.

B. **Wash your hands:** Always wash your hands before and after changing your menstrual product. This will help prevent the spread of bacteria and infection.

C. **Keep your genital area clean:** During your period, it's important to keep your genital area clean to prevent infection. You can do this by washing with warm water and mild soap.

D. **Choose the right menstrual products:** There are a variety of menstrual products available, including pads, tampons, menstrual cups, and period underwear. Choose the product that works best for your body and lifestyle.

E. **Avoid scented products:** Scented menstrual products, such as pads and tampons, can irritate your skin and disrupt your natural pH balance. Stick to unscented products to prevent irritation and infection.

By following these basic tips for menstrual hygiene, you can help prevent infection and stay comfortable during your period.

Here is a Guidelines on how to clean menstrual products and how often to change them:

Menstrual Product	Cleaning Instructions	How often to change
Disposable pads	Simply discard used pads in the trash	Every 4-6 hours, or more often if you have heavy bleeding
Tampons	Remove the used tampons and discard it in the trash. If using applicator tampons, dispose of the applicator as well	Every 4-6 hours, or more often if you have heavy bleeding. Never leave a tampon in for more than 8 hours
Menstrual cups	Remove the cup and empty the contents into the toilet. Rinse the cup with water and reinsert. Between periods, boil the cup in water for 5-10	Every 8-12 hours, or more often if you have heavy bleeding. Boil the cup between periods

	minutes to sanitize	
Period underwear	Rinse the underwear in cold water, then wash in the washing machine with regular laundry detergent. Avoid using fabric softener	Depending on the absorbency of the underwear, change every 4-6 hours or as needed

Remember, these are general guidelines and may vary depending on your individual flow and preferences. It's important to listen to your body and change your menstrual product as often as needed to maintain good hygiene and prevent leaks or infection.

Chapter Seven:

Periods and Sports

Many young girls and women may believe that their menstrual cycle prevents them from participating in sports or other physical activities. Periods, with the proper preparation and management techniques, should not interfere with athletic performance. In fact, regular exercise can help to alleviate menstrual symptoms and improve menstrual health overall. In this chapter, we will look at the effects of menstruation on athletic performance, the best ways to manage menstruation during sports, and some tips for staying comfortable and confident while exercising.

➢ Effects of periods on sports performance:

Periods are commonly thought to have a negative impact on athletic performance, but this is not always the case. While some women may experience cramping or discomfort during their period, studies have shown that there is no significant difference in athletic performance during menstruation compared to other times of the month. Individual experiences may differ, and some women may feel less energized or experience more severe menstrual symptoms during their period, which can have an impact on their athletic performance.

➢ Managing periods during sports:

There are several ways to manage periods during sports to ensure comfort and prevent leaks. One common method is to use tampons or menstrual cups, which are designed to be worn internally and provide greater freedom of movement compared to pads. It's also important to wear comfortable, breathable clothing that allows for unrestricted movement and prevents chafing. Additionally, it's a good idea to bring extra menstrual products and a change of clothes in case of any unexpected leaks.

➢ **Tips for staying comfortable and confident:**

For some girls and women, participating in sports during their period can be a source of anxiety or embarrassment. However, there are several tips and tricks to help stay comfortable and confident while staying active. One tip is to choose darker-colored clothing to prevent any visible leaks, or to wear a loose-fitting shirt or jacket for added coverage. Additionally, it can be helpful to practice good hygiene, such as washing your hands before and after changing your menstrual product, and using fragrance-free wipes or sprays to freshen up if necessary.

While periods can pose some challenges when it comes to participating in sports or other physical activities, they do not have to be a barrier to performance or enjoyment. With the right preparation and management techniques, it is possible to stay comfortable and confident while staying active. By understanding the effects of periods on sports performance, utilizing effective menstrual products, and practicing good hygiene and self-care, girls and women can continue to pursue their athletic goals and stay healthy and happy during their period.

Tips for Managing Periods while Participating in Sports:

Participating in sports can be difficult for women who have periods, especially if they have heavy bleeding, cramps, or other menstrual symptoms. However, with proper management and preparation, it is possible to continue participating in sports while on your period. Here are some suggestions for managing periods while participating in sports:

1. *Use the right menstrual product: Choosing the right menstrual product is important when participating in sports. Tampons or menstrual cups are recommended over pads as they are more secure and comfortable during physical activities. Choose a product with the right absorbency level based on your flow and change it frequently to prevent leaks and discomfort.*
2. *Wear comfortable clothing: Wearing comfortable clothing can make a huge difference in managing your period while*

participating in sports. Choose moisture-wicking and breathable fabrics that can help prevent discomfort and irritation. Also, consider wearing dark-colored clothing to hide any potential leaks.

3. ***Stay hydrated:*** *Drinking plenty of water is essential to staying hydrated while participating in sports, especially when experiencing menstrual symptoms such as cramps. Proper hydration can also help regulate your menstrual cycle and reduce bloating.*

4. ***Plan ahead****: Planning ahead is key to managing your period while participating in sports. Pack extra menstrual products, pain relievers, and any other necessary items in your sports bag. Also, consider scheduling your activities around your menstrual cycle to avoid discomfort and fatigue.*

5. ***Take breaks when necessary****: Taking breaks during physical activities can help manage menstrual symptoms such as cramps and fatigue. Listen to your body and take breaks when necessary to rest and recover.*

6. ***Practice good menstrual hygiene:*** *Proper menstrual hygiene is essential when participating in sports. Change your menstrual product frequently and wash your hands before and after changing it. Also,*

shower or bathe regularly to maintain good hygiene and prevent infections.

7. **Talk to your coach or trainer:** *If you feel uncomfortable or have concerns about managing your period while participating in sports, talk to your coach or trainer. They can provide support and advice on how to manage your period while continuing to participate in sports.*

In conclusion, managing periods while participating in sports requires proper planning, the right menstrual products, comfortable clothing, good menstrual hygiene, and staying hydrated. With these tips, it is possible to continue participating in sports while on your period.

Chapter Eight:

Periods and Mental Health

Puberty and adolescence can be a difficult time for many adolescent girls, with menstrual hormonal changes sometimes causing mental and emotional health issues. Periods can have a variety of effects on mental health, ranging from mild mood swings to severe anxiety and depression. Teens must be aware of how their periods can affect their mental health and learn coping mechanisms to deal with these effects.

Periods can cause changes in the levels of hormones such as estrogen and progesterone in the body, which can lead to mood changes and even depression. Teen girls may experience feelings of irritability, sadness, or anxiety, and these emotions can be overwhelming at times. It's essential to know that these feelings are valid and that there are ways to manage them effectively.

Furthermore, teens who have pre-existing mental health conditions, such as anxiety or depression, may have worsened symptoms during their menstrual cycle. It is critical to communicate with healthcare providers about any concerns regarding mental health symptoms so that they can recommend treatment options or make changes to current treatment plans.

It is also critical for adolescent girls to understand that they are not alone in their feelings. Many girls and women experience mental health changes during their periods, and it is critical that they communicate openly and support one another. Speaking with a trusted adult or mental health professional can help reduce feelings of isolation while also providing advice on how to manage period-related mental health symptoms.

In this chapter, we will discuss the various ways in which periods can impact mental health and provide tips on how to manage these effects. We will also cover the importance of seeking help if mental health symptoms become severe or interfere with daily life. It's important to remember that prioritizing mental health is just as crucial as physical health, and taking care of both can lead to a happier and healthier life.

➢ Health Concerns related to Teens

For many teenage girls, getting their periods can be a challenging experience that comes with various physical and emotional changes. Hormonal fluctuations during the menstrual cycle can significantly affect a girl's mood, behavior, and overall mental health. While some girls may not experience any negative emotional effects, others may face a range of mental health challenges that can be both uncomfortable and frustrating.

One of the most common mental health concerns related to periods is premenstrual syndrome (PMS). PMS is a collection of physical and emotional symptoms that occur in the days or weeks leading up to a girl's period. These symptoms can include mood swings, anxiety, depression, irritability, fatigue, and headaches. Some girls may also experience severe symptoms that interfere with their daily lives, a condition known as premenstrual dysphoric disorder (PMDD).

In addition to PMS, periods can also trigger or worsen existing mental health conditions such as anxiety and depression. Girls who already struggle with these conditions may find that their symptoms worsen during their periods. Hormonal changes during the menstrual cycle can disrupt the balance of chemicals in the brain, leading to negative emotional effects.

Furthermore, the stigma surrounding menstruation can also impact a girl's mental health. Many girls feel embarrassed or ashamed about their periods, leading to feelings of isolation or low self-esteem. They may also feel that their periods make them less attractive or that they need to hide their symptoms from others, which can further exacerbate their mental health concerns.

It's essential for teenage girls to understand that experiencing mental health challenges related to periods is normal and that there are various ways to manage these symptoms. Speaking openly with a trusted healthcare provider or mental health professional can be helpful in developing a plan to manage symptoms effectively. Additionally, practicing self-care techniques such as getting enough sleep, eating a healthy diet, and engaging in pysical activity can help alleviate symptoms.

Overall, it's essential for teenage girls to prioritize their mental health and seek help when needed. With the right support and resources, they can learn to manage their mental health challenges related to periods effectively.

> ## How Hormonal Changes during the menstrual cycle impact mood and Mental Health

The menstrual cycle is a complex physiological process that involves a series of hormonal changes. These hormonal changes can sometimes impact mood and mental health. The menstrual cycle is divided into four phases, each characterized by specific hormonal changes and physiological events. The first phase is the menstrual phase, which is when bleeding occurs. The second phase is the follicular phase, which is when the ovaries are preparing to release an egg. The third phase is the ovulatory phase, which is when the egg is released from the ovary. The fourth phase is the luteal phase, which is when the uterus prepares for possible implantation of a fertilized egg.

During the menstrual cycle, the levels of estrogen and progesterone fluctuate. These hormones play a crucial role in regulating the menstrual cycle and preparing the body for pregnancy. However, when there is an imbalance in these hormones, it can lead to mood changes and other mental health concerns.

Premenstrual Syndrome (PMS) is a common mental health concern related to hormonal changes during the menstrual cycle. PMS refers to a set of physical and emotional symptoms that occur in the week or two before menstruation. Symptoms can include mood swings, irritability, depression, anxiety, fatigue, bloating, and headaches. PMS can be caused by changes in the levels of estrogen and progesterone, which can affect the neurotransmitters in the brain that regulate mood.

Premenstrual Dysphoric Disorder (PMDD) is a more severe form of PMS. It affects up to 8% of menstruating women and is characterized by intense emotional and physical symptoms that can significantly impact daily life. Symptoms of PMDD can include severe mood swings, feelings of hopelessness, anxiety, panic attacks, irritability, anger, and fatigue. PMDD is thought to be caused by an abnormal response to the hormonal changes that occur during the menstrual cycle.

Depression and anxiety can also be related to hormonal changes during the menstrual cycle. Some women may experience an increase in symptoms of depression and anxiety during certain phases of their cycle, such as the luteal phase. These symptoms can be caused by changes in the levels of estrogen and progesterone, which can affect the levels of neurotransmitters in the brain that regulate mood.

Eating disorders can also be related to hormonal changes during the menstrual cycle. Some women may experience an increase in symptoms of an eating disorder, such as binge eating or purging, during certain phases of their cycle. These symptoms can be caused by changes in the levels of hormones that regulate appetite and food intake.

In conclusion, hormonal changes during the menstrual cycle can sometimes impact mood and mental health. It is important for women to be aware of the potential for these changes and to seek support if they are experiencing symptoms of PMS, PMDD, depression, anxiety, or an eating disorder. There are a variety of treatments available, including medication, therapy, and lifestyle changes, that can help manage these symptoms and improve overall mental health.

Tips for Managing and Coping with Mental Health during Periods:

Managing and coping with mood and mental health issues related to the menstrual cycle can be challenging, but there are several tips and strategies that can help:

i. **Keep track of your menstrual cycle**: Use a menstrual calendar or tracking app to record the timing and duration of your periods, as well as any symptoms or changes in mood you experience. This can help you anticipate and prepare for any mood changes that may occur during your cycle.

ii. **Practice self-care:** Engage in activities that help you feel calm and relaxed, such as yoga, meditation, deep breathing exercises, or taking a warm bath. Get plenty of rest and make sure you're eating a healthy, balanced diet.

iii. **Exercise regularly:** Regular exercise can help improve mood and reduce stress levels. Aim for at least 30 minutes of moderate exercise, such as brisk walking or jogging, several times a week.

iv. **Talk to someone**: If you're feeling overwhelmed or anxious, it can be helpful to talk to a trusted friend or family member, or a mental health professional. They can provide support and guidance as you navigate any mood or mental health issues you may be experiencing.

v. **Consider therapy:** Therapy can be an effective tool for managing mood and mental health issues related to the menstrual cycle. Cognitive-behavioral therapy (CBT) is a common approach that can help you identify and change negative thought patterns, as well as develop coping strategies for managing mood swings and other symptoms.

vi. **Try relaxation techniques:** Relaxation techniques such as progressive muscle relaxation, guided imagery, or aromatherapy can help reduce stress and anxiety, and improve mood.

vii. **Consider medication:** If your mood or mental health issues are severe, your doctor may recommend medication to help manage symptoms. Antidepressants, mood stabilizers, and hormonal contraceptives are all options that can help regulate mood and manage symptoms of PMS and PMDD.

It's important to remember that everyone's experience with periods and mental health is unique, and what works for one person may not work for another. Experiment with different coping strategies and seek professional help if you need it. With time and patience, it is possible to manage and improve your mental health during your menstrual cycle.

Conclusion

Period books for teen girls have grown in popularity over the years as an essential guide for girls navigating the changes in their bodies during puberty. These books provide insights into the physical and emotional changes that occur with the onset of menstruation, as well as practical advice on how to deal with this difficult time in a girl's life.

In recent years, there has been a growing emphasis on destigmatizing menstruation, and period books for teen girls play a vital role in achieving this goal. These books help girls understand that menstruation is a normal and natural part of the female reproductive cycle and provide them with the information they need to manage their periods with confidence and ease.

One of the most important advantages of period books for adolescent girls is that they offer an open and honest forum for discussing menstruation. Girls can feel more comfortable discussing their concerns and seeking advice from trusted sources if they talk openly about menstruation. Furthermore, by reading books about menstruation, girls can learn about other girls' experiences and realize they are not alone in their struggles.

Period books for teen girls also provide valuable information about menstrual products, including pads, tampons, and menstrual cups. By learning about the different products available, girls can choose the best option for their needs, and feel more confident about managing their periods. Furthermore, these books can help girls understand the importance of hygiene during menstruation and provide practical advice on how to maintain good hygiene during this time.

Another significant benefit of period books for teen girls is that they help girls understand the emotional changes that accompany puberty. Many girls experience mood swings, anxiety, and depression during puberty, and these books can provide valuable insights into these emotional changes. By understanding that these changes are a natural part of the process, girls can feel more comfortable discussing their feelings and seeking help when needed.

Period books for teen girls also serve as an essential tool for parents and caregivers. By providing these books to their daughters, parents can help them prepare for puberty and provide them with the information they need to manage their periods. Furthermore, these books can help parents initiate discussions about puberty and menstruation, which can be challenging for some parents.

In conclusion, period books for teen girls are a valuable resource for girls who are navigating the changes in their bodies during puberty. These books provide practical advice on managing periods, destigmatize menstruation, and offer insights into the emotional changes that accompany puberty. By reading these books, girls can feel more confident about managing their periods, and parents can feel more comfortable discussing puberty and menstruation with their daughters. Ultimately, period books for teen girls help girls transition from childhood to adolescence with greater ease and confidence. One of the most important advantages of period books for adolescent girls is that they offer an open and honest forum for discussing menstruation. Girls can feel more comfortable discussing their concerns and seeking advice from trusted sources if they talk openly about menstruation. Furthermore, by reading books about menstruation, girls can learn about other girls' experiences and realize they are not alone in their struggles. One of the most significant advantages of period books for adolescent girls is that they provide an open and honest forum for discussing menstruation. Girls can feel more comfortable discussing their concerns and seeking advice from trusted sources if menstruation is discussed openly. Furthermore, by reading books about menstruation, girls can learn about the experiences of other girls and realize that they are not alone in their struggles.

Made in the USA
Coppell, TX
02 November 2023

23720193R00056